Praise for Mastering Me...

"The daily themes remind women that self-mastering is necessary for sound living. Mastering Me is a must-read "can-do" devotional steeped in word and truth!"
—Natoya Walker Minor, Deputy General Manager Greater Cleveland Regional Transit Authority

"*Mastering Me* is an inspirational, insightful, and relevant journal for women in search of encouragement. LaToya compiled life-saving and life-changing nuggets that will expand your thinking."
—Dr. Terence O. Hayes, Sr., pastor, author, and girl dad

"If you have ever experienced doubt, disappointment, or fear (and who hasn't?), you will find transformation in the pages of Mastering Me. With truth and transparency, LaToya courageously shares her life experiences in a way to which every woman can relate. This book offers practical tools based on biblical principles that will equip you to replace fear with faith."
—Karen M. R. Townsend, Ph.D., women's empowerment expert

"Women of faith must spend time excavating the precious gems obtained in the kiln of everyday life. In *Mastering Me*, LaToya skillfully takes you on a journey of self-discovery, self-reflection, and ultimately, self-mastery. Using Scriptures and relevant personal examples, she encourages women to discover purpose and embrace their God-given gifts. No matter how long you've walked with God, you will find this devotional challenging and refreshing. Every woman needs this book as she seeks the MASTER to master all she is destined to do."
—Dr. Matisa Wilbon, founder of Women of a Higher Call

Mastering Me

A 30-Day Devotional for

Christian Women

By
LaToya D. Masterson

Published by

Queen V Publishing
Englewood, OH
QueenVPublishing.com

Published by
Queen V Publishing
Englewood, OH
QueenVPublishing.com

Copyright © 2022 by LaToya D. Masterson

All rights reserved. No part of this book can be reproduced in any form without written permission from the author.

The author guarantees all writings are original works and do not infringe upon the legal rights of any other person living or deceased.

All Scriptures are from NKJV unless otherwise noted.

Library of Congress Catalog Number: 2022902175

ISBN-13: 978-1-7358162-0-3

Edited by Valerie J. Lewis Coleman of Pen of the Writer

Proofread by Sharahnne Gibbons of Something in Comma

Author photo by Rebecca Valentine of InksByCheRee Photography

Printed in the United States of America

This book is dedicated to every woman pursuing unfulfilled dreams, purpose, and self-discovery.

Acknowledgements

I first acknowledge my Lord and Savior, Jesus Christ. Thank You for salvation, guidance, and birthing this book in me.

My parents: James and Eva Masterson. Thank you for loving me and pushing me to be the best version of myself. You remind me that success has no limits, and everything is possible with faith and hard work.

Bishop Eugene Ringer, my father in the Gospel and spiritual hero. Thank you for believing in me and equipping me with a solid spiritual foundation.

My POWER Team: Rae'Sean Jones, Alisha Hayes-Bonner, Yolanda Munguia, and Jade Bonner. Thank you for supporting me on my writing journey. With my best interest at heart, you gave honest feedback and recommendations. I could not have completed this project without you.

My family and friends, thank you for words of encouragement, love, prayer, and support. Your influence helped form me into the woman I am today.

My sisters in the Bookish Book Club. You dope women inspired me to take risks and pursue my dreams.

My publisher and editor, Valerie J. Lewis Coleman. From start to finish, working with you was done in the spirit of excellence. Thank you for your guidance, feedback, and transparency. This dream would have been unmet without your expertise.

Table of Contents

Introduction 11
Day 1 *I'm Running Out of Time* 13
Day 2 *Should I Give Thanks?* 17
Day 3 *To Change or Not to Change?* 21
Day 4 *I'm Not Strong Enough* 27
Day 5 *Well, Well, Well* 31
Day 6 *You Can* 35
Day 7 *Help in the Fire* 39
Day 8 *Strong Foundation* 43
Day 9 *Why?* 47
Day 10 *Ready, Set, Go!* 51
Day 11 *Wrong Direction* 55
Day 12 *God's Grace* 59
Day 13 *Car Trouble* 63
Day 14 *When Opportunity Knocks* 67
Day 15 *Favor* 71
Day 16 *Too Many* 75
Day 17 *Who Is in Your Circle?* 79
Day 18 *In That Very Hour* 83
Day 19 *Yet Will I Trust Him* 87
Day 20 *Take Another Look* 91

Day 21 *Promises*	95
Day 22 *You Should Be a Witness*	101
Day 23 *What are You Thinking?*	105
Day 24 *Prayer & Praise*	109
Day 25 *It's Never Too Late*	113
Day 26 *Salt*	117
Day 27 *Detour*	121
Day 28 *Most Needful*	125
Day 29 *Ready or Not, Here I Come*	129
Day 30 *I AM THAT I AM*	133
About LaToya D. Masterson	137
About Queen V Publishing	139

Introduction

Do you have an unfilled dream? Are you unsure of your purpose? If you answered yes to either question, this devotional is for you.

On the journey to self-discovery and purpose, you will experience fears, doubts, and obstacles. In those moments, you may want to question God. "Lord, where are You?" or "Why am I going through this?" If you are like me, you wanted to throw in the towel and quit during those challenging times.

This devotional was birthed from a time when God pushed me to see my life from His perspective. He needed me to change my thoughts, remember His promises, and trust Him completely. I am often reminded of Job's faith in the midst of adversity.

Though He slay me, yet will I trust Him.
—Job 13:15

I wrote this devotional to encourage and challenge you to keep dreaming and pursuing purpose. When you encounter uncertainty, remember God just needs you to seek Him, believe, and stand on your faith. He will take care of the rest.

For I know the thoughts that I think toward you, says the Lord, thoughts of peace and not of evil, to give you a future and a hope.
—Jeremiah 29:11

Because I want you to experience transformation, I included reflection activities at the end of each devotional. Ponder and pray. Write your thoughts, heart matters, and God's inspirations in the space provided.

My prayer is that you
- Find your strength in God.
- Experience a mindset shift to see yourself as He sees you.
- Witness God at work in every situation.

And we know that all things work together for good to those who love God, to those who are the called according to His purpose.
—Romans 8:28

This journey is preparation for your unique purpose and divine destiny. Faith and fear cannot occupy the same space. Be blessed.

LaToya D. Masterson

Day 1

I'm Running Out of Time

Time is of the essence especially when deadlines are fast approaching and immediate attention is required. The matter seems so urgent that if it's not done on time, the results will be catastrophic possibly unto death.

For the last three years, I completed a vision board prior to the start of the year. My vision boards consist of images and words that represent the goals, desires, and dreams I hope to manifest. Last year, my vision board included images of a

- Devotional representing this 30-day devotional. Done!
- Stage overlooking an audience in anticipation of obtaining John Maxwell certification as speaker, trainer, and coach. Done!
- Bible with the words "Lord, increase my hunger for Your Word and decrease my hunger for this world." This image reflected aligning with God's will for me and opened doors in ministry. Done!

Although the fourth goal did not manifest, Habakkuk 2:2-3 reminded me that a written vision is for an appointed time. Your timing may not align perfectly with God's, but wait for the vision to manifest.

At a certain season, an angel troubled the water at the Pool of Bethesda. The first person to step into the troubled water was healed of sickness and disease. A man had an infirmity for almost four decades but had no one to help him into the pool. I'm sure he wondered if his time would ever come. When Jesus saw the man, He said, "Will you be made whole?" The man assumed that his healing was tied to being first in the pool and told Jesus that someone always stepped in front of him because he didn't have help getting into the water. Jesus didn't ask about stepping into the water. He wanted to know if the man had faith to be healed regardless of the water, failed attempts, and timing.

Take three deep breaths. You are still alive, which means that you still have time to live your best life. God came so that you could experience abundant life. You may become frustrated, disturbed, or upset when things don't go as planned. In those moments, I encourage you to remember God's Word. Ecclesiastes Chapter 3 is a great reminder that every situation has a specific God-ordained time and season. He made everything beautiful — in His perfect timing — and wants only the best for you. Delay is not denial, it's just not yet. Relax. God has your back.

As noted in 2 Peter 3:8, a thousand years to man is one day to God. In man-time, what seems like forever is just a blink of His eye.

> *There is a time for everything, and a season for every activity under the heavens: He has*

made everything beautiful in its time. He has also set eternity in the human heart; yet no one can fathom what God has done from beginning to end.
—Ecclesiastes 3:1; 11

For I know the thoughts that I think toward you, says the Lord, thoughts of peace and not of evil, to give you a future and a hope.
—Jeremiah 29:11

Now a certain man was there who had an infirmity thirty-eight years. When Jesus saw him lying there, and knew that he already had been in that condition a long time, He said to him, "Do you want to be made well?"
—John 5:5-6

Reflection Activity

Read Ecclesiastes 3:1-11. What does the passage mean to you?

_____

_____

_____

_____

How can you apply this reflection to your life?

_____

_____

_____

_____

_____

What other Scriptures bring you peace in times of chaos?

_____

_____

_____

_____

_____

Think about a time you waited for God to answer a prayer. What did you learn as you waited?

_____

_____

_____

_____

_____

Day 2

Should I Give Thanks?

When I lived with my parents, I woke up one morning with excruciating chest pain. On a scale of one to ten, the throbbing pain tipped the scale. I thought I was having a heart attack. I screamed for help and asked my parents to call the ambulance. As we waited, my mother prayed. She thanked God for healing despite my agonizing pain. She stood in the gap when I couldn't stand for myself. The pain intensified and I wondered if God was listening. Thanking Him was the furthest thing from my mind.

The paramedics hooked me to a heart monitor, gave me oxygen, and transported me to the hospital. The lab work, x-rays, EKGs came back normal. The pain subsided, but without a diagnosis, my mind was not at rest. At the follow-up appointment, my physician ordered a hepatobiliary iminodiacetic acid (HIDA) scan. The result? I had a bad gallbladder and over one hundred gallstones! Once the root cause was identified, corrective measures were taken. I thank God for my praying mother, attentive medical personnel, and God's healing.

When Jesus passed through Samaria and Galilee, He encountered ten lepers. With contagious painful sores all over their bodies, lepers were deemed unclean. To keep everyone safe, they were isolated away from town. The lepers cried for Jesus to have mercy on them. Testing their faith, He told them to see the priest, a ritual started by Moses (Leviticus 13). All ten were healed of leprosy, but only one man returned to thank Jesus. For his faith and gratitude, Jesus took his physical healing to the next level. He restored his spirit man, thus making him whole.

Should you give thanks even when you don't feel thankful? Absolutely! He wants you to give thanks in everything: the good, bad, and ugly. Despite His perceived delayed answer, unchanged circumstances, or how you feel, your responsibility is to manage your perspective. You can be optimistic, joyful, and hopeful during uncertainty. Replace anxiety with prayer and thanksgiving. Be intentional about developing an attitude of thankfulness and not just for the "big" things. Express appreciation for a parking spot near the entrance, lights that work when you flip on the switch, and new mercies to do His work. You will confuse the enemy, disrupt his power, and turn your trouble into triumph.

> *God is not human, that He should lie, not a human being, that He should change His mind. Does He speak and then not act? Does He promise and not fulfill?*
> —Numbers 23:19

Be anxious for nothing, but in everything by prayer and supplication, with thanksgiving, let your requests be made known to God;
—Philippians 4:6

In everything give thanks; for this is the will of God in Christ Jesus for you.
—1 Thessalonians 5:18

Reflection Activity

Take a few minutes to reflect on what you are thankful. List what comes to mind.

_____
_____
_____
_____
_____

Throughout the day, give thanks for the items on your list.

_____
_____
_____
_____
_____

Tonight, reflect on how your thankfulness affected your attitude and actions.

_____
_____
_____
_____
_____

How can you incorporate daily thankfulness going forward?

_____
_____
_____
_____
_____

Day 3

To Change or Not to Change?

You experience change in the workplace with a new boss, fired co-worker, or different hours. The air in your home circulates every hour and your HVAC works to regulate the fluctuating temperature. Your body generates new hair every two to seven years, skin every twenty-seven days, and blood cells every second.

December 2013, I was called to the ministry. This major life change brought fear and uncertainty. As I thought about *my* plans, I wanted to run away from the call. In my mind, the burden was too much to carry. But, when I gathered my thoughts and focused on God's plan for me, I committed to share His message. As I prayed, He equipped me for the journey. I released my will to follow His. I changed my thoughts, my words, and my actions. I became a willing vessel used by God to introduce transformation to His children.

In Acts 9, Saul threatened and slaughtered the Lord's disciples. On the road to Damascus, a light shone from heaven and Saul fell to the ground. An omnipresent voice questioned why he persecuted Him. Saul realized this encounter was supernatural and acknowledged that the Lord spoke to him. Saul was blinded by the presence of God and received instruction about how to have his sight restored. This man, who fought against God and His people, had a change of heart. After his sight was restored, he was baptized, filled with the Holy Ghost, and served as one of Christ's disciples. Because of his transformation, his powerful ministry brought salvation to others.

Change is inevitable, so why resist it so relentlessly? Because stepping outside of your comfort zone can be scary, frightening to the point of paralysis. Living in the realm of status quo is easy. You know the routine; you know what to expect. But in that realm, you don't leave room for God to mature you or bless you. Instead of looking at change as a bad thing, consider it as an opportunity to grow and learn. What's on the other side of change? Better health, less stress, improved relationships, more money…peace!

Are you avoiding change? If God asked you to trust Him to do a new thing in your life, He has already ordered your steps. You don't have to fear the unknown, which is only unknown to you. If you wait for full understanding, proof, or confirmation to take action, you may miss all that God has planned for you. Change is coming. How you respond dictates your results.

> *And the Lord, He is the One who goes before you. He will be with you, He will not leave you nor forsake you; do not fear nor be dismayed.*
> —Deuteronomy 31:8

Mastering Me

Trust in the Lord with all your heart, and lean not on your own understanding; in all your ways acknowledge Him, And He shall direct your paths.
—Proverbs 3:5-6

Behold, I will do a new thing, now it shall spring forth; shall you not know it? I will even make a road in the wilderness and rivers in the desert.
—Isaiah 43:19

Reflection Activity

Describe your Damascus Road experience.

_____

_____

_____

_____

_____

How does change make you feel?

_____
_____
_____
_____
_____

Do you need to make a change or decision that requires you to step out on faith?

_____
_____
_____
_____
_____

If so, what is keeping you from taking the first step?

_____
_____
_____
_____
_____

Mastering Me

What can you do today to act on Proverbs 3:5-6?

_____

_____

_____

_____

LaToya D. Masterson

Day 4

I'm Not Strong Enough

In 2018, my place of employment closed...permanently. As a leader, I was responsible for informing employees of the inevitable shutdown. The burden of the affected families settled on my shoulders and weighed on my heart. Although the situation was not my fault, delivering such devastating news caused anxiety. I cried. I questioned. I felt like I was losing my mind. I feared for them, their families, and myself. I didn't have the strength to continue.

God reminded me of David and Goliath. Armed with a slingshot, five stones, and unwavering faith, David confronted the giant. The first stone struck and killed Goliath. No sword, no shield, just faith. What the entire Israelite army could not do, God did through a ruddy shepherd boy.

I gathered my weapons: prayer, fasting, and the Word. I trusted God to handle the rest. He was my strength. He shielded my peace. You don't have to rely on your strength because with God, you are strong enough.

> *Come to Me, all you who labor and are heavy laden, and I will give you rest.*
> —Matthew 11:28

And He said to me, "My grace is sufficient for you, for My strength is made perfect in weakness." Therefore most gladly I will rather boast in my infirmities, that the power of Christ may rest upon me.
—2 Corinthians 12:9

I can do all things through Christ who strengthens me.
—Philippians 4:13

Reflection Activity

Read 1 Samuel 17 to learn about David's defeat over the Philistine giant, Goliath.

Recall a test or trial you felt you weren't strong enough to handle. Did you make it through? What actions did you take?

_____
_____
_____
_____
_____

What comes to mind when you read 2 Corinthians 12:9?

_____

_____

_____

_____

_____

Write a situation that has you feeling like your strength is failing. Cross through the situation and then add the affirmation: I can do all things through Christ who gives me strength.

_____

_____

_____

_____

_____

LaToya D. Masterson

What other Scriptures strengthen you in times of weakness?

_____

_____

_____

_____

_____

Day 5

Well, Well, Well

First impressions can lead—or mislead—you. At the onset of business meetings, I form opinions about those in attendance. A few years ago, I attended a leadership conference in Atlanta. I connected with a fellow leader who was ecstatic about growth and development. We networked and exchanged leadership tidbits. My first impression led me to a professional relationship that was mutually beneficial. In another instance, I worked with an acquaintance to host an event. We had problems with coordination, resource availability, and trust. When we talked about the issues, miscommunication and misperception were corrected. We had the same goal; however, first impressions misled my thinking.

The assumption reminded me of the story of the Samaritan woman. As she drew water from the well, Jesus asked her for a drink. Since Jews had no dealings with Samaritans, she assumed He had ulterior motives and questioned Him. She had no idea that the Savior of the world stood before her. Jesus, in His gentleness, told her that He was the gift of God, able to give her living water. He had an everlasting supply that fueled mind, body, and soul. She almost missed her eternal blessing based on an inaccurate assumption rooted in tradition.

LaToya D. Masterson

How many times have you drawn conclusions, excluded people, or dismissed an opportunity from God like the woman at the well? Be open to encounters with Jesus, whether in your quiet time, encouraging words from a friend, or the actions of a stranger. His well is designed to give you abundant everlasting life, but you have to tap into the source.

> *Then they said to Him, "What shall we do, that we may work the works of God?" Jesus answered and said to them, "This is the work of God, that you believe in Him whom He sent."*
> —John 6:28-29

> *The thief does not come except to steal, and to kill, and to destroy. I have come that they may have life, and that they may have it more abundantly.*
> —John 10:10

> *Do not forget to entertain strangers, for by so doing some have unwittingly entertained angels.*
> —Hebrews 13:2

> *And this is the testimony: that God has given us eternal life, and this life is in His Son.*
> —1 John 5:11

Mastering Me

Reflection Activity

Read John 4:7-14. What does this passage teach you about Jesus? About the Samaritan woman? About yourself?

_____
_____
_____
_____
_____

Describe three times when you were like the woman at the well.

_____
_____
_____
_____
_____

LaToya D. Masterson

Share your woman-at-the-well moments with the Lord. Ask for His forgiveness and guidance to avoid missing opportunities to bless or be blessed.

_____

_____

_____

_____

_____

Day 6

You Can

Since as long as I can remember, I wanted to work in healthcare. I have always been passionate about caring for others and helping them in times of uncertainty.

As a college freshman, a family emergency forced me to miss the anatomy and physiology final. I scheduled the make-up with my instructor and learned that the second-chance test was not multiple choice like the original. The make-up exam was essays, which were much more difficult. Despite the long hours I spent preparing and studying, I failed the final. Devastated.

I made an appointment with the instructor to determine my next steps. As we reviewed my answers, I noticed that I did not get credit for answers that were conceptually the same as the book.

My unkind instructor said, "Your answers are not exactly how it is written in the book. You are not cut out to be a nurse."

In a state of shock and crushed to my core, my mind raced. Words escaped me as feelings of doubt, inadequacy, and failure consumed me. I hurriedly left my instructor's presence. As I paced, my parents' words echoed in my head. "There is nothing you cannot do when you put your mind to it." I knew that I was called to serve. I knew that failures had embedded lessons. I affirmed that I am who God says I am and that I can do all things through Christ because He is my strength. I needed to surround myself with teachers who believed in me, so after finishing the semester, I transferred to a different college. It was the best decision I ever made. I obtained my nursing license in 2003 and have worked in the field ever since.

In 1 Samuel 16, God sent Samuel to anoint one of Jesse's sons as king of Israel. After seven sons came before Samuel, he asked Jesse, "Are these all of your children?" Jesse overlooked his youngest son, David, who was busy doing his father's business, shepherding the flock. When David arrived, the Lord told Samuel to anoint him. Ruddy, brave, smelly David was destined to be king and a man after God's own heart. Man looks at the outward appearance, while God looks at your heart.

No one can determine, detour, or disregard the destiny God has set before you but you. No more evil thoughts or false witness. Believe in yourself. Believe in what God has spoken over you! You can be whatever you desire.

> *For as he thinks in his heart, so is he. "Eat and drink!" he says to you, but his heart is not with you.*
> —Proverbs 23:7

"Before I formed you in the womb, I knew you; before you were born I sanctified you; I ordained you a prophet to the nations."
—Jeremiah 1:5

But those things which proceed out of the mouth come from the heart, and they defile a man. For out of the heart proceed evil thoughts, murders, adulteries, fornications, thefts, false witness, blasphemies.
—Matthew 15: 18-19

I can do all things through Christ who strengthens me.
—Philippians 4:13

Reflection Activity

Write about a time someone told you that you could not do something. How did you feel? What was your response?

_____
_____
_____
_____
_____

What did you learn from that experience?

_____
_____
_____
_____
_____

Who does God say you are?

_____
_____
_____
_____

Remember, recite, and recall this Scripture when you feel like you can't:

> *For I know the thoughts that I think toward you, says the Lord, thoughts of peace and not of evil, to give you a future and a hope.*
> —Jeremiah 29:11.

Day 7

Help in the Fire

Sometimes it feels like you are bombarded with one test after the other. As soon as you have things figured out, here comes something else. Feelings of being overwhelmed and consumed try to overtake you to admit defeat.

A friend shared things she was dealing with personally, emotionally, and spiritually. She was overwhelmed with life and felt consumed by its devices. She had unpaid bills, disconnect notices, deadlines for schoolwork, and a minor health issue. On top of her personal challenges, she bore the weight of others' problems, because she was dubbed "the strong one." Deflated and defeated, she could not see a way out.

Those deemed strong seldom decompress and share their feelings. So instead of offering advice, I listened, granting her some relief from the burdensome weight. I encouraged her with God's promises of being a present help, protector from the enemy's fiery darts, and provider who would never leave or forsake her.

In Daniel 3, King Nebuchadnezzar decreed that when his music played, every man had to bow down and worship a golden image. Anyone who defied the king's order would be cast into a fiery furnace. Committed to serving the one true and living God, the three Hebrew boys did not obey the decree. When confronted for insolence, they stood firm, believing that if God did not deliver them, He was still able. They were thrown into the furnace and the king commanded the soldiers to increase the fire seven times. Expecting the boys to be burned to ashes, Nebuchadnezzar was astonished when he saw four men walking in the fire. The Hebrew boys were not consumed, neither did a flame touch their skin and clothing. They did not even smell of smoke. They experienced no remnant or residue of the king's failed attempt to destroy them. Because they believed, God honored their faith by joining them in the fire. God will do the same for you during your fiery-furnace experience.

Advice like "don't focus on the circumstance" or "it is not as bad as it looks" offers little consolation. In those moments, stand on His Word. He is an omnipresent help in the time of trouble. He is omnipotent, all powerful. His strength prevails especially in your weakness. He can do anything, anytime, anywhere, and any way He chooses. Nothing is impossible for Him.

> *God is our refuge and strength, a very present help in trouble.*
> —Psalm 46:1

Through the Lord's mercies we are not consumed, because His compassions fail not. They are new every morning. Great is Your faithfulness.
—Lamentations 3:22-23

For with God nothing will be impossible.
—Luke 1:37

And He said to me, "My grace is sufficient for you, for My strength is made perfect in weakness." Therefore most gladly I will rather boast in my infirmities, that the power of Christ may rest upon me.
—2 Corinthians 12:9

Reflection Activity

Are you experiencing an all-consuming matter? Are you so overwhelmed that you cannot focus, rest, or pray?

_____

_____

_____

_____

_____

What Scriptures can you apply to the situation?

_____
_____
_____
_____
_____

Write the Scriptures on index cards or an app in your phone. When the enemy tries to overtake you, read the Scriptures out loud, bind the enemy's attempts, and ask God to help you.

Day 8

Strong Foundation

Memorial Day 2019 began as a great day barbequing and hanging out with my family and friends. After a full day of food, fun, and fellowship, I lay down about 11:00 pm. A few minutes later, my aunt called.

"Take cover! They just issued a tornado warning!"

Alone and afraid, I ran downstairs to take cover in the bathroom. As the winds howled and my house shook, the wind rumbled and roared as the tornado passed. I cried out to God for protection. What seemed like forever, was only a few moments. When the house stopped swaying and the wailing stopped, I ran upstairs to assess the damage. At first glance, nothing was broken or missing. I called loved ones to make sure they were okay. Although everyone was fine, I couldn't fall asleep wondering what I would find when the sun rose.

At least one of fifteen tornadoes whipped near my neighborhood. The next morning, I noticed damage to my roof and siding. Leaves and small branches of neighbors' trees were in my yard. Thank God for His protection and homeowner's insurance.

The most destructive tornado was upgraded to EF4 due to winds and damage. Three-fifths of a mile wide, it traveled twenty miles staying on the ground about thirty minutes.[1] It snatched houses from foundations, and ripped trees out of the ground. Massive trees with exposed roots lay in yards and blocked streets. According to GovTech.com, 2,550 homes and 173 businesses were affected. To date, some of the damaged structures have not been repaired or replaced.[2]

In Luke 6:46-49, Jesus illustrated the stability of building on a solid, sturdy foundation. Obeying His words is like building on a foundation of rock that can withstand storms. However, choosing to live without Christ is like building on sand. A splash of water will wash away the foundation and a storm will demolish everything.

As I thought about how quickly devastation occurred, it reminded me of life's tribulations. If you are not careful, circumstances can overtake you and destroy your foundation. Build your foundation on Jesus Christ. He is always with you. When storms come—and they will come—Jesus is the solid rock; a foundation that will not be shaken. Use the authority He gave you to command the storm to be still.

---

[1] *15 Memorial Day Tornadoes Confirmed; EF4 Traveled 20 Miles, Over Half-Mile Wide;* https://www.whio.com/news/local/ef3-tornado-confirmed-beavercreek/vjklb2LUNZvmtyj78jNaZN. Accessed online 10.05.21.

[2] *Tornadoes Destroy More Than 600 Homes in One Ohio County;* https://www.govtech.com/em/disaster/montgomery-county-ohio-tornadoes-left-more-than-600-homes-unlivable.html. Accessed online 10.05.21.

Mastering Me

Therefore thus says the Lord God, "Behold, I lay in Zion a stone for a foundation, A tried stone, a precious cornerstone, a sure foundation; Whoever believes will not act hastily.
—Isaiah 28:16

And I also say to you that you are Peter, and on this rock I will build My church, and the gates of Hades shall not prevail against it.
—Matthew 16:18

Then He arose and rebuked the wind, and said to the sea, "Peace, be still!" And the wind ceased and there was a great calm.
—Mark 4:39

Reflection Activity

Read Luke 6:46-49. Write your thoughts as you read that passage.

_____
_____
_____
_____
_____

What do you think caused the instability when your foundation wavered during life's storms?

_____

_____

_____

_____

_____

How did you feel standing on shaky ground?

_____

_____

_____

_____

_____

What steps can you take to make sure your foundation is strong, solid, and sturdy?

_____

_____

_____

_____

_____

Day 9

Why?

Why am I here? Why me? Why not me? Why is everyone against me? Why doesn't someone love me the way I want to be loved? Why? Why? Why?

It is natural to wonder why things happen, especially when you don't know the purpose. Diamonds are formed far beneath Earth's surface. Heat, pressure, and time are required to create these beautiful, precious stones. Although the process may be painful, difficult, and frustrating, God is working it for your good. You may feel like a hidden gem, but the pressure will not destroy you. It may seem like forever, but time is critical to your process. God is forming you into the woman He needs to draw others to Him. He is preparing you for kingdom ministry. Your process has not gone unnoticed. People are watching your transformation as you conquer each why. Your testimony of tragedy-to-triumph will shift the lives of others.

One afternoon in March 2020, I stopped by Family Dollar for a few household items. As I approached the counter, I noticed the coughing cashier looked flustered. I was a bit skeptical given COVID, but he had on a mask, so I completed my purchase and left. A few days later, I had a pounding migraine which shot down my back. Between coughs, I experienced shortness of breath. Night sweats drenched my bed. My doctor confirmed that I had COVID. At first, I panicked. I wondered what I did wrong to contract the virus because I followed all the recommended precautions: social distancing, masking, sanitizing my hands, and staying home unless going to the store or work. My doctor gave me vitamins and medicines to take while I isolated myself for two weeks. With the virus being new, unfamiliar, and broadcasted on every media channel, I was scared. I prayed. God comforted me, calmed my fears, and increased my faith.

In the book of Ruth, Naomi's husband and two sons died. Naomi encouraged her daughters-in-law, Ruth and Orpah, to return to their homelands. After a brief discussion, Orpah, left. Ruth insisted on staying with Naomi and stated her devotion in Ruth 1:16. I'm convinced this duo questioned why God took their men, property, and livelihood, but they kept pressing. Naomi mentored Ruth on the customs of her people, explained the laws, and positioned her to work in the fields of a relative, Boaz. As Ruth worked to provide food for Naomi and herself, Boaz, the wealthy kinsmen redeemer, noticed her. With guidance from Naomi, a gentle heart, and kind spirit, Ruth won his heart. He married her, restoring her natural inheritance and positioning her in the bloodline of Christ. God used a situation filled with whys, to restore everything that was lost.

Don't be distracted by why. Change your "why me" to what is God trying to teach to me. Learn the lesson in the pressing so you don't have to march around the same mountain for years.

> *Many are the afflictions of the righteous, but the Lord delivers him out of them all.*
> —Psalm 34:19

> *He has made everything beautiful in its time. Also He has put eternity in their hearts, except that no one can find out the work that God does from beginning to end.*
> —Ecclesiastes 3:11

> *We are hard-pressed on every side, yet not crushed; we are perplexed, but not in despair; persecuted, but not forsaken; struck down, but not destroyed.*
> —2 Corinthians 4:8-9

> *And they overcame him by the blood of the Lamb and by the word of their testimony, and they did not love their lives to the death.*
> —Revelation 12:11

LaToya D. Masterson

Reflection Activity

Read Ruth. What aspect of that book resonates most with you?

_____
_____
_____
_____
_____

What whys weigh heavy on you?

_____
_____
_____
_____

Ask God for His purpose for each situation.

What does 2 Corinthians 4:8-9 mean to you?

_____
_____
_____
_____
_____

Day 10

Ready, Set, Go!

In middle school, I asked my parents if I could run track. At the first practice, the coaches instructed the team to run a route with lots of hills and turns. I started strong, looked like a champion. However, as the highs-and-lows and twists-and-turns kept coming, I tired and eventually sat on the ground to recover. All my teammates passed me. About twenty minutes later, still sitting on the ground, my father came to help. He was worried because I had not crossed the finish line with the other runners. I decided that track was not for me.

Mark 5:25-34 tells about the woman with the issue of blood. For twelve years, she suffered with a blood issue. She spent all of her money looking for a cure, but no relief came…until Jesus. When she learned that Jesus was coming, she mustered the strength to press through the crowd to touch the hem of His garment. Putting action to her faith not only healed her, it stopped Jesus in His tracks. He wanted to see the woman who had faith in His healing power. He found her in a sea of people and affirmed her with internal peace and external healing. My God!

Sometimes it feels like you are running for your life. And if you're not prepared, dedicated, or motivated, you may want to "sit this one out." The peaks and valleys of life get hard, but don't quit. Take a break if you must, but stay in the race. God's Word says that it's not about speed or strength. The winner is the one who endures the tough times to finish. He said that you are more than a conqueror, so you will win! Get ready, set, go!

> *I returned and saw under the sun that — the race is not to the swift, nor the battle to the strong, nor bread to the wise, nor riches to men of understanding, nor favor to men of skill; but time and chance happen to them all.*
> —Ecclesiastes 9:11

> *No weapon formed against you shall prosper, and every tongue which rises against you in judgment you shall condemn. This is the heritage of the servants of the Lord, and their righteousness is from Me," says the Lord.*
> —Isaiah 54:17

> *But he who endures to the end shall be saved.*
> —Matthew 24:13

> *"Teaching them to observe all things that I have commanded you; and lo, I am with you always, even to the end of the age." Amen.*
> —Matthew 28:20

Mastering Me

Yet in all these things we are more than conquerors through Him who loved us.
—Romans 8:37

Reflection Activity

What characteristics are essential to win a race?

_____

_____

_____

_____

Which of those characteristics do you have? Need to improve?

_____

_____

_____

_____

Preparing for a marathon requires training your mind, body, and soul. You need the right running shoes, support bra, and attire. What you put in your body is just as important as what you put on your body. And the mental preparation, whew! Think about your life today and where you want to be in the future. What goals to want to achieve in the next month? Next year? Three years?

_____

_____

_____

_____

_____

What do you need to do now to be ready next month? Next year? Three years?

_____

_____

_____

_____

_____

When things get hard, what Scriptures motivate you to finish your race?

_____

_____

_____

_____

Day 11

Wrong Direction

One year, I traveled with my family to Alabama for a family reunion. The gathering was held at an unfamiliar park filled with long roads lined with tall trees. We didn't see any landmarks or road signs to figure out if we were going the right way. I whipped out my cell phone to Google the directions. Despite being deep in the woods, I got a decent signal and found the route. We went a few miles when the connection dropped. Lost without written directions or GPS navigation, I hit the OnStar button in my truck. With a more powerful signal, we connected to a reliable source, and arrived safely.

For forty years, the children of Israel wandered in the wilderness. Their journey to the Promised Land should have taken eleven days, but murmuring, complaining, and disobedience extended the walk to four decades. Despite witnessing God's miracles and experiencing His presence as a pillar of cloud by day and flame by night, they let unbelief and disobedience hinder their progress to the promise. Once they reached their destination, Moses sent twelve spies to search Canaan. Ten returned with a bad report because they were afraid of the giants who occupied the land. However, Joshua and Caleb, the other two spies, believed that they could overtake the inhabitants to possess the land because the Lord was with them. Even with God's backing and this favorable report, the children of Israel refused to trust God. To their detriment, they experienced God's wrath. Everyone twenty years and older died in the wilderness without receiving the promise. If the children of Israel had followed God's lead, they would have bypassed decades of wasted wandering and lived the abundant life He wants for all of us.

If you have ever felt lost, at a loss for words, misplaced, or no sense of self, one of the first responses is to find your way. You search for ways to express your feelings, belong, and find yourself. After many attempts of trying the do-it-yourself way, you realize that a more reliable connection is necessary. The Word says that God is our source and resource. He is the connection—the missing link—that will lead you in the right direction.

> *I will instruct you and teach you in the way you should go; I will guide you with My eye.*
> —Psalm 32:8

> *Trust in the Lord with all your heart, and lean not on your own understanding; in all your ways acknowledge Him, and He shall direct your paths.*
> —Proverbs 3:5-6

Mastering Me

For in Him we live and move and have our being, as also some of your own poets have said, 'For we are also His offspring.'
— Acts 17:28

Reflection Activity

Read Numbers Chapters 13-14 to understand the defiant children of Israel.

Think of a time when you tried repeatedly to correct something, but nothing worked. What happened when you let God lead the way?

_____

_____

_____

_____

_____

What did you learn from that situation?

_____

_____

_____

_____

LaToya D. Masterson

What can you do to strengthen your connection with God, so your first thought is to let Him lead?

_____

_____

_____

_____

_____

Day 12

God's Grace

Driving home one evening, I fell asleep at the wheel. I hit a yield sign, the car swerved, and jarred me awake. I was headed into a tree, when the car stopped abruptly. I don't remember slamming on the brakes. With minimal damage to the car and zero personal injury, I knew God protected me in the near-death experience.

In John 8, the Scribes and Pharisees caught a woman committing adultery and brought her to Jesus. Sidebar: I never understood why they didn't bring the man with whom she committed the sin. They did not like the attention Jesus had received and tried to snare Him by asking His opinion of the Law of Moses which condemned her to death by stoning. They didn't understand that Jesus came to fulfill the law and replace its punishment with grace.

Jesus stooped to doodle in the dirt like He didn't hear them. They persisted questioning Him and accusing the woman, until Jesus stood and said, "He who is without sin among you, let him throw a stone at her first." He stooped to doodle again. Not one of the accusers was blameless and able to condemn the woman. They walked away leaving Jesus and the woman. He showed her grace by pardoning her sin and instructed her to not sin anymore.

LaToya D. Masterson

Justice is getting what you deserve. Mercy is not getting what you deserve. Grace is getting what you do not deserve. How often do you think about God's grace? Where would you be if it had not been for His unmerited favor? God bankrupted heaven to give His only begotten Son so you could have abundant life. His grace is sufficient, or enough, to protect and keep you from dangers seen and unseen. Since He freely gives you grace and mercy, extend that favor to others, even when you feel they don't deserve it.

> *For God so loved the world that He gave His only begotten Son, that whoever believes in Him should not perish but have everlasting life.*
> —John 3:16

> *But God demonstrates His own love toward us, in that while we were still sinners, Christ died for us.*
> —Romans 5:8

> *And God is able to make all grace abound toward you, that you, always having all sufficiency in all things, may have an abundance for every good work.*
> —2 Corinthians 9:8

Mastering Me

And He said to me, "My grace is sufficient for you, for My strength is made perfect in weakness." Therefore most gladly I will rather boast in my infirmities, that the power of Christ may rest upon me.
—2 Corinthians 12:9

Reflection Activity

How have you experienced the grace of God?

_____
_____
_____
_____

If not for His unmerited favor, where would you be?

_____
_____
_____
_____

LaToya D. Masterson

How can you show grace to others?

_____

_____

_____

_____

Day 13

Car Trouble

Due to the pandemic, I worked remotely from home with a weekly trip to the office. On one such trip, my car would not start. Panic. I called AAA to assess my car and give me a jump. Once he got the car started, the technician instructed me to let it run for at least forty-five minutes to charge the battery. He told me that I need to replace the battery as soon as possible. I tried several places, but none could assist me because I needed a shop with a battery saver. Otherwise, when replaced, all the car's memory including mileage, speed-and-breaking patterns, seatbelt usage, and airbag deployment would be lost. I called the dealership where I purchased the car and made an early appointment for the next day. Guess what. The next morning, my car refused to start. When panic tried to overtake me again, something inside of me said, "Lay hands on your car and pray. Speak life to your dead battery." I did and less than a minute later, my car started.

In Ezekiel 37, God placed Ezekiel in a valley of dry bones. He asked the prophet, "Can these bones live?" When Ezekiel said, "Only You know," the Lord told him to prophesy to the bones and command them to live. Because of Ezekiel's obedience, the bones lived.

What dead things are wasting away in your life? God gave you power and authority to speak life to revive them. By combining your faith, words, and works, you can shift anything. His Word is life. He made you in His image and gave you dominion over earthly things. If He can bring the dead to life, you can, too. No matter what you are facing, pray, speak His Word, and watch Him breathe life into it.

> *Then the Lord God formed a man from the dust of the ground and breathed into his nostrils the breath of life, and the man became a living being.*
> —Genesis 2:7

> *Death and life are in the power of the tongue, and those who love it will eat its fruit.*
> —Proverbs 18:21

> *The Spirit of God, who raised Jesus from the dead, lives in you. And just as God raised Christ Jesus from the dead, he will give life to your mortal bodies by this same Spirit living within you.*
> —Romans 8:11

> *Even so the tongue is a little member and boasts great things. See how great a forest a little fire kindles!*
> —James 3:5

Mastering Me

Reflection Activity

Read Ezekiel 37:1-14. What does the passage mean to you?

_____

_____

_____

_____

_____

Think about the "dead" things in your life. Write them in the space provided.

_____

_____

_____

_____

_____

Pray, speak, and command them to live according to God's will.

LaToya D. Masterson

How did God revive those dead things?

_____

_____

_____

_____

_____

Day 14

When Opportunity Knocks

Early in my nursing career, a supervisor approached me with a promotion opportunity on a different unit. My immediate response, "No, thanks." Fear, doubt, and lack of confidence combined with a bad experience as a floater on the unit resulted in a hasty decision. Thankfully, my supervisor was persistent. The second time she proposed the position, my mind was open to the possibility. I stepped out on faith into the unknown and it was the best decision of my life. The experience was a steppingstone into leadership and God's purpose for me.

Queen Esther had the opportunity to speak on behalf of her people so that they would not be killed. Her initial response was triggered by fear because law dictated that she could not access the king—her husband—without being summoned. Her uncle, Mordecai, reminded her that if she remained silent, God would raise up another deliverer.

According to Esther 2:12, the king's wives and concubines had to spend twelve months of beautification before they could access him. This matter was too urgent for delay. Esther gathered the people, called a fast, and declared that she would go before the king even if it cost her life. Because she put faith over fear, her people were saved. God's plan was fulfilled as a result of Esther's obedience to an opportunity.

Are you contemplating an opportunity? Before you make a decision, assess the pros and cons, talk to God, and wait for His direction. He may be trying to reveal another part of His plan for you. Opportunities are often presented when you least expect them.

> *So Samuel said: "Has the Lord as great delight in burnt offerings and sacrifices, as in obeying the voice of the Lord? Behold, to obey is better than sacrifice, and to heed than the fat of rams.*
> —1 Samuel 15:22

> *"Before I formed you in the womb I knew you; before you were born I sanctified you; I ordained you a prophet to the nations."*
> —Jeremiah 1:5

> *For I know the thoughts that I think toward you, says the Lord, thoughts of peace and not of evil, to give you a future and a hope.*
> —Jeremiah 29:11

> *Now faith is confidence in what we hope for and assurance about what we do not see.*
> —Hebrews 11:1

Reflection Activity

Read Esther 4. How does the passage have relevance in your life?

_____
_____
_____
_____
_____

What opportunities have you turned down that you wish you hadn't?

_____
_____
_____
_____
_____

What kept you from taking that opportunity?

_____
_____
_____
_____
_____

LaToya D. Masterson

Looking back on missed opportunities, what did you lose? Gain?

_____

_____

_____

_____

_____

What will you do differently when opportunity knocks? Why?

_____

_____

_____

_____

Day 15

Favor

Following an amazing celebration for my cousin's fiftieth birthday, my family and I headed back to the US. When we got to the Belize airport, we learned that our flight had been delayed due to technical issues. Since we had the last connecting flight out of Houston, I was concerned, especially when they pushed back the departure time...twice! As with all international flights, they screened our bags upon entering the US. As a result, we had to claim the bags, recheck them, and then go back through TSA. At baggage claim, we encountered another delay. The passing storm ushered in thunder, lightning, and rain so the crew could not safely unload baggage. Over the loudspeaker, a calming voice indicated that connecting flights for international passengers would be held. Whew! About forty minutes later, we got our bags and sprinted through the terminal. The gate attendant told us that the flight had left ten minutes ago. I was upset. We did everything they told us to do, yet they still left us. We talked with an airline agent who apologized for the inconvenience. As compensation, they provided lodging in a five-star hotel, three meals, and an upgrade to first class, which was a new experience for me. Nice. What seemed like a setback to my plan, was the favor of God in His plan.

LaToya D. Masterson

The most favored of Jacob's twelve sons, Joseph was envied and hated by his brothers. They threw him into a pit and conspired to kill him but sold him into slavery instead. He was unjustly thrown into prison where God's unmerited favor kept him. When no one else could interpret Pharaoh's dream, Joseph deciphered it finding favor with the king of Egypt. Joseph was elevated to second-in-command responsible for preparing for the coming famine. Ultimately, Joseph delivered his family from starvation, and they lived out their lives protected by the king. Despite the betrayal, abandonment, and struggle, Joseph remained content and steadfast. His pit-to-palace-to-prison-to-palace experience had God's favor all over it.

As a child of the King of kings, His favor dominates your life. Every morning, He gives you new mercies. He protects you from dangers you don't even know exist. He has purpose for you and makes provision to fulfill it. Regardless of what comes against you, be like Joseph: know your calling, operate in faith, and forgive those who offend you.

But the LORD was with Joseph and showed him mercy, and He gave him favor in the sight of the keeper of the prison.
—Genesis 39:21

Mastering Me

Therefore, my beloved brethren, be steadfast, immovable, always abounding in the work of the Lord, knowing that your labor is not in vain in the Lord.
—1 Corinthians 15:58

Now godliness with contentment is great gain.
—1 Timothy 6:6

Reflection Activity

Read Joseph's story in chapters 37, 39-41 of Genesis.

How did you handle hurt inflicted by family, friends, or church members?

_____

_____

_____

_____

_____

How did God's favor help you through the experience?

_____
_____
_____
_____
_____

What steps can you take to be content in all things?

_____
_____
_____
_____
_____

Day 16

Too Many

I attended a team building exercise at the Escape Room. With the clock ticking, we had one hour to solve puzzles, crack codes, and find hidden items to escape. It didn't take long for us to realize that we were all over the place. Several team members barked comments at the same time. We missed the clues "hidden in plain sight" because we jumped in without a plan. Fifteen minutes wasted, we stopped to strategize. Everyone stepped back to let those best suited take the lead. We failed to escape in the allotted time; however, we learned a valuable lesson: more isn't always better.

God wanted to use Gideon, a mighty man of valor, to deliver Israel from the Midianites. But Gideon doubted himself—and God—because he gathered 32,000 men to fight with him. God told Gideon that he had too many men and instructed him to let those who were fearful return home. With 10,000 men remaining, Gideon was ready for battle, but in so many words, God said, "Not so fast." Gideon had to complete one more test to reduce the number of warriors. He watched as the men drank water from a nearby stream. Those who put their face in the water to lap like dogs were excused. The three hundred men who knelt putting hand-to-mouth were chosen for war because they drank and watched.

Why did God reduce the head count? If the 32, 000-man army had won the battle, they would have boasted that they did it of their own strength.

Not everyone can go where God wants to take you. Whether they're afraid, prideful, or ill equipped, they could hinder your deliverance. Seek God for discernment. Ask Him how to conquer your battle instead of depending on the strength of others. God wins every battle, and He waits to win yours. Obey Him, trust Him, and you will be victorious.

> *The Lord will fight for you, and you shall hold your peace.*
> —Exodus 14:14

> *For the Lord your God is He who goes with you, to fight for you against your enemies, to save you.*
> —Deuteronomy 20:4

> *Then the Lord said to Gideon, "By the three hundred men who lapped I will save you, and deliver the Midianites into your hand. Let all the other people go, every man to his place."*
> —Judges 7:7

Mastering Me

Reflection Activity

Read Judges 6:11-16; 7:3-7. What did the passage mean to you?

_____

_____

_____

_____

What battles are you facing today?

_____

_____

_____

_____

Who's in your corner? Water-walking-faith-filled friends or fearful ones?

_____

_____

_____

_____

LaToya D. Masterson

Ask God for discernment on which steps to take and with whom. Write His revelations to you.

_____

_____

_____

_____

_____

Day 17

Who Is in Your Circle?

My family and friends say that I don't meet strangers and no matter where I go, I know someone there. They might just be right because I am intentional about being friendly as described in Proverbs 18:24. However, despite all the people I know, my inner circle is small. I have a few select friends I can call when I need help. They pray, fast, and give me encouragement or correction when needed, and I do the same for them. True friendship.

Luke 5 tells of a young man who was stricken with palsy, a form of paralysis often accompanied with involuntary tremors. He wanted to get to Jesus, but the pressing crowd—and his condition—made it impossible. His friends hoisted him to the rooftop, cut a hole in the roof, and lowered him to Jesus. Jesus forgave his sins and healed his body!

Anyone can stand by your side when things are easy and going well. You need friends who will do what it takes to help you get healing, deliverance, and breakthrough. Assess your inner circle. It may be time for a change.

> *A friend loves at all times, and a brother is born for adversity.*
> —Proverbs 17:17

LaToya D. Masterson

A man who has friends must himself be friendly, but there is a friend who sticks closer than a brother.
—Proverb 18:24

When He saw their faith, He said to him, "Man, your sins are forgiven you."
—Luke 5:20

Reflection Activity

Read and reflect on Luke 5:17-25. What does this passage teach you about friendship?

_____

_____

_____

_____

_____

Who can you call on when you need help?

_____

_____

_____

_____

How do you know you can depend on them?

_____
_____
_____
_____
_____

How can you be the type of friend in the passage?

_____
_____
_____
_____

LaToya D. Masterson

Day 18

In That Very Hour

One morning about two o'clock, I woke with excruciating abdominal pain. Paralyzed with pain, tears flowed. I didn't move fearing the slightest movement would worsen the pain. My mind raced as to what to do and who to call. I prayed. I reminded God that He promised in Isaiah 53:5 that His stripes can heal me. Five minutes later, the pain subsided, and I exhaled.

Jesus had been on a healing crusade when a centurion, a Roman commander of one hundred men, met Him at Capernaum. The military leader asked Jesus to heal his servant who was at home sick and tormented. Jesus told the man that He would go with him to heal his servant. Full of selflessness, the centurion did not feel worthy to have Jesus at his house, so he asked Him to speak a word to heal his servant. Jesus marveled at his faith and healed the servant that very hour.

Jesus is no respect of persons. Just like the centurion, you can walk in humility, elevate your faith, and manifest His promises. Look beyond your present circumstances and rename the situation. Unlock the keys of the Kingdom to bind the enemy and loose God's blessings. Bind sickness and disease. Loose healing. Bind anxiety. Loose peace. Bind lack. Loose abundance. Go boldly to the throne of grace, ask Him to speak a word over your situation, and then put action with your faith. Try it and watch God move!

> *Jesus Christ is the same yesterday, today, and forever.*
> —Hebrews 13:8

> *Thus also faith by itself, if it does not have works, is dead.*
> —James 2:17

> *Therefore humble yourselves under the mighty hand of God, that He may exalt you in due time.*
> —1 Peter 5:6

Reflection Activity

Read Matthew 8:5-13. What comes to mind when you read about the centurion?

_____

_____

_____

_____

_____

Mastering Me

In what areas can you put your faith to work?

_____

_____

_____

_____

_____

Read Matthew 18:18-20. Create your bind-loose statements and read them aloud daily.

_____

_____

_____

_____

_____

LaToya D. Masterson

Day 19

Yet Will I Trust Him

In 2020/21, pandemic, racial tension, natural disasters, and death afflicted the world like never before.

As a veteran healthcare professional, my faith was tested daily. I had never witnessed so much sickness and death in my eighteen years of service. The volume of COVID patients was at an all-time high. Teams were exhausted. People could not visit dying loved ones because of restrictions in place to slow the spread of virus. Heartbreaking. Added to stressors inherit with the job, I took extra precautions to ensure the safety of family and friends. After God, relationships are next in importance to me. I isolated myself from them in case I was infected at work. I missed our pre-pandemic Sunday dinners and often felt empty. I asked God to fill the void because even in adversity, He is still in control.

Job was an upright man chosen by God to exemplify trust and patience. With permission from God, Satan attacked Job with all he had. Limited only to not killing Job, the enemy took his children, wealth, and health. Painful oozing boils covered him from the soles of his feet to the crown of his head. No one is immune from suffering, but few could endure with competence like Job. His wife told him to curse God and die. His friends offered "support," but only brought negativity. Did he grieve? Absolutely, but he never lost faith. When others would have crumbled, Job worshipped. Even when he felt that the torment would lead to death, he trusted God. Not only did Job's actions shame the enemy, the Lord rewarded him with a double portion of blessings.

No matter what fiery darts the enemy sends your way, know that he can only do what God allows. The Father may be testing your faith or teaching you a lesson. In the midst of adversity, trust Him, worship Him, and ask Him what He wants you to learn.

> *Though He slay me, yet will I trust Him. Even so, I will defend my own ways before Him.*
> —Job 13:15

> *And the Lord restored Job's losses when he prayed for his friends. Indeed the Lord gave Job twice as much as he had before.*
> —Job 42:10

> *For I consider that the sufferings of this present time are not worthy to be compared with the glory which shall be revealed in us.*
> —Romans 8:18

> *If we endure, we shall also reign with Him. If we deny Him, He also will deny us.*
> —2 Timothy 2:12

Mastering Me

Reflection Activity

Read Job 1:6-12. What does the passage mean to you?

_____

_____

_____

_____

_____

How do you respond during times of suffering?

_____

_____

_____

_____

_____

On the other side of suffering, what did you learn about God? Yourself?

_____

_____

_____

_____

_____

How can you show God that you trust Him in all things?

_____

_____

_____

_____

_____

Day 20

Take Another Look

About five o'clock one morning, I drove to work. The thick fog made it difficult to see lane lines, stop signs, and oncoming traffic. Moving with slow, steady precision, I managed to make it out of the complex. At the stop sign to the main road, I looked left and right. Darkness. I signaled my intention with the left blinker and eased out slowly. When I looked to the right, I saw a car barreling toward me. Given the low visibility, this driver was moving way too fast. I slammed on my brakes. If hadn't taken another look, a collision would have been inevitable. Since most car accidents happen within ten miles from home, I pray for traveling mercies every time I get into my car, not just long-distance trips, and ask God for protection from seen and unseen dangers. My life was spared because I took another look.

The blind man at Bethsaida had a life-changing encounter with Jesus. He begged Jesus to heal him. Jesus showed care, compassion, and consideration as He took the blind man by the hand and guided him around obstacles to a place away from the crowd. Jesus spit on his eyes, placed His hands on him, and asked him what he saw. When he said, "I see men as trees walking," Jesus laid His hands on him again and told him to look up. With another look, the blind man was completely restored.

Why did Jesus touch him twice? Some teach that the two-touch miracle was an illustration of how man sees but does not understand (spiritual blindness). Others teach that the man's limited faith affected his complete healing. Still others indicate that the process of physical and spiritual healing is not always instantaneous, thereby requiring the recipient to remain steadfast and unmovable. Whatever your school of thought, know that Jesus did not fail with the first touch. And He will not fail you.

Can you imagine Jesus leading you? Directing you over and around obstacles. Although it may be difficult, step out of your situation and assess it from a different perspective...God's eagle-eye view. Understanding that He is genuinely concerned about your physical and spiritual development brings clarity and focus. Seek Jesus diligently, follow His instruction, and take another look.

> *I will lift up my eyes to the hills – from whence comes my help?*
> —Psalm 121:1

> *Then He touched their eyes, saying, "According to your faith let it be to you."*
> —Matthew 9:29

> *For He healed many, so that as many as had afflictions pressed about Him to touch Him.*
> —Mark 3:10

Reflection Activity

Read Mark 8:22-26. What did you learn about the persistent blind man? Jesus?

_____
_____
_____
_____

What areas of your life seem unclear?

_____
_____
_____
_____

How does this passage encourage you to see things clearer?

_____
_____
_____
_____

LaToya D. Masterson

Day 21

Promises

A promise is a commitment that you will do — or not do — what you said. Honoring your word by following through on a promise builds relationships, credibility, and trust. On the contrary, breaking a promise breeds contention, tarnishes your name, and annihilates trust.

I promised God that I would walk according to His will. I have fallen short of that promise on a few occasions, but His unfailing love restored me. As a college student, a classmate broke a promise, betraying my trust and damaging our friendship. She hurt me to my core. Years later, the sting of betrayal angered me. The thought of her raised the hairs on the back of my neck. I realized that if I wanted His forgiveness for my wrongs, I had to exercise forgiveness toward her. I'm thankful that He graced me with time and a willing heart.

I analyzed my part in the situation. I was intentional about pleasing God and being at peace with my nemesis. As He promised in Proverbs 16:7, He made my enemies at peace with me. I released the offense and the emotions that came with it. I forgave her and asked God to bless her with His best. The next time I saw her, my neck hairs stayed in place. I didn't grimace, roll my eyes, or walk away. I knew that God had changed me.

If you don't think you can keep a promise, save yourself heartache and frustration by making it known upfront. Once the damage is done, it can take years—or never—to mend.

I know the ultimate promiser keeper. All of His promises are guaranteed when you meet His conditions:
- Ask Him. 2 Chronicles 7:14; Matthew 7:7-8; James 4:2-3
- Love Him. Deuteronomy 6:5; Joshua 23:11; Mark 12:30
- Keep His commandments. John 14:15-31
- Love others. 1 John 4:7-8
- Forgive others. Matthew 6:14-15; 1 John 1:9

In uncertain times, stand on the promises of God and be confident that they will manifest…in His timing. Because God is not a man, He does not have the ability to lie. He swears by Himself (Hebrews 6:13) because none greater exists. He has His own back when it comes to honoring His Word (Matthew 24:35). If He said it, then it will happen. Period.

Many Christians fall short because they do not intimately know the Lord. Study the Word, know His character, trust His promises, and activate your faith…in that order.

Fear not, for I am with you; be not dismayed, for I am your God. I will strengthen you, yes, I will help you, I will uphold you with My righteous right hand.
—Isaiah 41:10

For with God nothing will be impossible.
—Luke 1:37

Therefore if the Son makes you free, you shall be free indeed.
—John 8:36

For all the promises of God in Him are Yes, and in Him Amen, to the glory of God through us.
—2 Corinthians 1:20

Who Himself bore our sins in His own body on the tree, that we, having died to sins, might live for righteousness — by whose stripes you were healed.
—1 Peter 2:24

Reflection Activity

Read these God-cannot-lie Scriptures: Numbers 23:19; 1 Samuel 15:29; Psalm 89:35; Hebrews 6:18.

How does it feel knowing that He does not have the ability to go back on His Word?

_____

_____

_____

_____

_____

What promises have God spoken over your life?

_____

_____

_____

_____

_____

Do you believe the promises of God will come to pass?

_____

_____

_____

_____

_____

Mastering Me

What promises has God already fulfilled in your life?

_____

_____

_____

_____

_____

What can you do as you wait on the promises of God?

_____

_____

_____

_____

_____

Have you ever had someone break a promise to you?

_____

_____

_____

_____

_____

LaToya D. Masterson

How did it make you feel?

_____

_____

_____

_____

_____

Day 22

You Should Be a Witness

My family and I are going through a self-study Bible course. An eye-opening lesson for me was about witnessing and winning souls. I reflected on my life to evaluate the effectiveness of my witness.

In 2010, a dear friend battled a terminal disease. When I visited her in the hospital she said, "I am scared. Will you pray for me? I don't have a relationship with God like you do." My heart ached because I knew God's desire is to have a relationship with all of us. I wondered if I had taken time to share with her the good news of God before that moment. I took her by the hand and prayed for her salvation based on Acts 2:38-39 and Romans 10:9-10.

I instructed her to repeat after me.

"Lord, I believe that You are the only true and living God. I invite You into my life. Please forgive my sins. Fill me with Your Spirit. Release divine healing—spiritually, emotionally, and physically—into the atmosphere. Thank You for adopting me into Your family. In the matchless name of Jesus, amen."

She died; however, I am comforted knowing that she gave her life to the Lord.

The blind man in John 9 was healed by Jesus. The Pharisees questioned him because they did not agree with Jesus working—aka healing folks—on the

Sabbath. They asked the healed man if Jesus was a sinner. He said,

> "Whether He is a sinner or not, I do not know. One thing I know: that though I was blind, now I see."
> —John 9:25

What a powerful witness! The goodness, faithfulness, grace, and mercy of Jesus should pour out of everything you do. The Father sent His only begotten Son for your salvation. He wants to have an intimate relationship with you for eternity. You can draw others — family, friends, and strangers — to Him by your witness, words, and works. Your reward for faithful witness is His blessings on earth and a crown of righteousness in heaven.

Have your words and/or actions drawn others to Christ? Spread the good news of Jesus. Tell others who He is to you. Show them who He is by demonstrating the fruit of the Spirit.

> *The fruit of the righteous is a tree of life, and the one who is wise saves lives.*
> —Proverbs 11:30

> *For God so loved the world that He gave His one and only Son, that whoever believes in Him shall not perish but have eternal life. For God did not send His Son into the world*

to condemn the world, but to save the world through Him.
—John 3:16-17

But the fruit of the Spirit is love, joy, peace, forbearance, kindness, goodness, faithfulness, gentleness and self-control. Against such things there is no law.
—Galatians 5:22-23

Now there is in store for me the crown of righteousness, which the Lord, the righteous Judge, will award to me on that day – and not only to me, but also to all who have longed for His appearing.
—2 Timothy 4:8

Reflection Activity

Read John 9. What did the passage mean to you?

_____

_____

_____

_____

_____

How effective is your witness?

_____

_____

_____

_____

_____

What testimony can you share to help someone connect with Christ?

_____

_____

_____

_____

_____

What steps can you take to be a more effective witness?

_____

_____

_____

_____

_____

Share the good news of Jesus with someone today.

Day 23

What are You Thinking?

"Whether you think you can or cannot, you're right."
—Henry Ford

The desire to write a devotional for Christian women was birthed in me a few years ago, but fear overtook me. I doubted whether I could articulate my journey. I'm a nurse, not a writer. I sabotaged myself before I even started. About a year later, I attended a Pen of the Writer workshop hosted by Valerie J. Lewis Coleman. What a great experience! I learned about writing, publishing, and the journeys of other authors. My thoughts shifted from "I can't do this" to "One day, I will write a devotional." Near the beginning of the COVID-19 pandemic, I joined a book club. Through readings, discussions, and laughter, I shared my desire to write a devotional with my newfound sisterhood. Once I spoke it out loud, thoughts followed. I put words to paper as they encouraged and held me accountable. You are reading the book that my stinking thinking determined was out of reach.

Apostle Paul willingly endured suffering and persecution as he worked for the Lord. He practiced what he preached and challenged believers to rejoice in Christ and set aside worry. In Philippians 4:8-9,

Paul encouraged thinking on the things of God. His words empower and direct you to see beyond your current circumstances. As promised in Isaiah 26:3, God will keep you in perfect peace if you keep your mind on Him.

Thoughts are powerful because they influence your beliefs, attitudes, actions, and reactions. Thinking creates a chain reaction—thoughts-words-actions-habits-character-destiny—that sets you up for success or failure. Since everything starts with a thought, be mindful to guard your thoughts especially during times of uncertainty. Otherwise, negativity, doubt, and discouragement can burden you with unnecessary weight.

God promised that His peace will keep your heart and mind. Your part is to be intentional about what you think. Reject the bad and focus on the good to demolish stinking thinking. Change your thoughts, change your life. Start now!

> *For as he thinks in his heart, so is he. "Eat and drink!" he says to you, but his heart is not with you.*
> —Proverbs 23:7

> *Do not conform to the pattern of this world, but be transformed by the renewing of your mind. Then you will be able to test and approve what God's will is—His good, pleasing, and perfect will.*
> —Romans 12:2

> *Casting down arguments and every high thing that exalts itself against the knowledge of God, bringing every thought into captivity to the obedience of Christ.*
> —2 Corinthians 10:5

> *And the peace of God, which surpasses all understanding, will guard your hearts and minds through Christ Jesus. Finally, brethren, whatever things are true, whatever things are noble, whatever things are just, whatever things are pure, whatever things are lovely, whatever things are of good report, if there is any virtue and if there is anything praiseworthy – meditate on these things.*
> —Philippians 4:7-8

Reflection Activity

Have your thoughts ever gotten the best of you? Explain.

_____
_____
_____
_____
_____

Why is it important to guard your thoughts?

_____
_____
_____
_____
_____

Create I-am affirmations based on who God says you are. For example, I am wonderfully made. I am chosen by God. I am loving. I am worthy of love. Post them on your mirror, hang them on your refrigerator, and write them in your phone. Recite them out loud daily.

_____
_____
_____
_____
_____

What else can you do to change your thinking as noted in Philippians 4:7-8?

_____
_____
_____

Day 24

Prayer & Praise

My pastor, who was very dear to me, died October 2021. I had been under his tutelage for thirty years and considered him my earthly hero. The Sunday after he died, I was asked to minister. Bound by grief, I wanted to curl up in a ball and mourn alone. Everything inside of me wanted to decline, but then I remembered my pastor's faithfulness, dedication, and vow to the Lord. I knew that God would comfort, heal, and give me what the congregation needed. I listened to praise and worship music and prayed while tears flowed. The compassionate God heard my cries. He directed me to Psalm 121:1-2 and gave me an encouraging word: Look up! Your help comes from the Lord. Even in grief, you do not have to be bound because your freedom lies in Him.

While preaching and teaching about Jesus, Paul and Silas encountered a young lady with a spirit of divination. She followed them many days taunting in an effort to hinder their ministry work. Fed up with the evil spirit, Paul commanded it to come out of her and she was freed of the tormenting spirit. Because her masters profited from her divination, they were upset about her deliverance. Paul and Silas were beaten, bound with chains, and thrown into prison. But Paul and Silas did not let their imprisonment stop them. They prayed and sang praises to God, which got His attention. An earthquake shook the foundation of the prison opening doors, loosening shackles, and freeing captives.

God can send an earthquake into your situation to shake off what has you bound. Elbert Hubbard said, "When life gives you lemons, make lemonade." I say, "When life gives you problems, make prayer and praise priority."

> *I will lift up my eyes to the hills — from whence comes my help? My help comes from the Lord, who made heaven and earth.*
> —Psalm 121:1-2

> *Therefore if the Son makes you free, you shall be free indeed.*
> —John 8:36

> *For there is no partiality with God.*
> —Romans 2:11

> *And this she did for many days. But Paul, greatly annoyed, turned and said to the spirit, "I command you in the name of Jesus Christ to come out of her." And he came out that very hour.*
> —Acts 16:18

Reflection Activity

Read Acts 16:16-40. What are your thoughts about this passage?

_____

_____

_____

_____

_____

What things have you bound, imprisoned, or held hostage?

_____

_____

_____

_____

_____

LaToya D. Masterson

Change the narrative of those situations by attaching prayer and praise until God answers.

_____

_____

_____

_____

_____

Day 25

It's Never Too Late

I wanted to be certified as a John C. Maxwell speaker and leadership development coach. The first time I attempted the training, I had competing priorities on the job, at church, and at home. I could not understand why God didn't give me the desires of my heart, then it hit me. God's timing was a delay, not denial. Despite my disappointment, I thanked Him. Two years later, the opportunity came to pursue my certification. My schedule was less hectic, so I had adequate time to prepare and study. As a bonus, the two-year lag brought leadership experiences that helped me better relate to the content. The timing was perfect, and I obtained my certifications!

Lazarus, the brother of Mary and Martha, fell ill. They sent for Jesus; however, He delayed His arrival for two days. In the meantime, Lazarus died. Jesus, knowing His beloved friend was dead, told the disciples that Lazarus was asleep and He needed to awaken him. As Jesus approached, Martha stopped grieving to tell Him that He was too late to save her brother who had been in the tomb for four days. After a brief exchange, Jesus clarified Martha's misunderstanding by saying, "I am the resurrection and the life: he who believes in Me, though he was dead, yet shall he live."

You may not understand why you're going through, but know that delay is not denial. Like Job and the Hebrew boys understood, no matter the outcome, God is able. Although it may not seem like it, He is never late. When you believe, He can resurrect, restore, and revive every dead situation.

> *To everything there is a season, a time for every purpose under heaven:*
> —Ecclesiastes 3:1

> *"If that is the case, our God whom we serve is able to deliver us from the burning fiery furnace, and He will deliver us from your hand, O king. But if not, let it be known to you, O king, that we do not serve your gods, nor will we worship the gold image which you have set up."*
> —Daniel 3:17-18

> *We are hard-pressed on every side, yet not crushed; we are perplexed, but not in despair.*
> —2 Corinthians 4:8

Reflection Activity

Read Ecclesiastes 3:1-15, Daniel 3, and John 11:1-40. What do these passages reveal to you about God's ability and timing?

_____

_____

_____

_____

_____

What goals, aspirations, or desires have you given up on because you thought it was too late to accomplish?

_____

_____

_____

_____

_____

Since it's never too late, what can you do today to move closer to achieving it?

_____

_____

_____

_____

_____

Create an action plan with incremental goals: 30 days, 60 days, 90 days, etc. to convert your desired outcomes into small, manageable steps.

_____

_____

_____

_____

_____

Day 26

Salt

One Sunday after church, my family went out to eat. I ordered a grilled chicken meal with loaded mashed potatoes. My mouth watered with anticipation when the server put the visually stunning plate in front of me. I couldn't wait to bite into the potatoes but was disappointed when they hit my taste buds. Bland. I don't have high-blood pressure and did not request a low-sodium meal, but that's what I got. I added salt and enjoyed my meal.

In addition to enhancing flavor, salt can be used to preserve food, cleanse, and relieve soreness when it's stored properly. Jesus said that you are the salt of the earth. You have been favored by God to flavor the world with His savory message of abundant life. In Mark 9:49-50, Jesus emphasized that salt is good. Much like salt, you are a preserving agent who enhances those around you. Make a positive difference and draw others to Christ.

You must be properly stored in prayer and relationship with God so that you don't lose your savor—aroma, enjoyment, passion—for Kingdom living. Sprinkle some salt, share your light, and hold onto to your savor.

"You are the salt of the earth; but if the salt loses its flavor, how shall it be seasoned? It is then good for nothing but to be thrown out and trampled underfoot by men. You are the light of the world. A city that is set on a hill cannot be hidden."
—Matthew 5:13-14

But you shall receive power when the Holy Spirit has come upon you; and you shall be witnesses to Me in Jerusalem, and in all Judea and Samaria, and to the end of the earth."
—Acts 1:8

Let your speech always be with grace, seasoned with salt, that you may know how you ought to answer each one.
—Colossians 4:6

Draw near to God and He will draw near to you. Cleanse your hands, you sinners; and purify your hearts, you double-minded.
—James 4:8

Mastering Me

Reflection Activity

Why do you think Jesus warned you to not lose your savor?

_____

_____

_____

_____

_____

What steps are you taking or need to take to maintain your savor?

_____

_____

_____

_____

_____

How can you be salt and light to the world?

_____

_____

_____

_____

_____

LaToya D. Masterson

Day 27

Detour

As a creature of habit, I travel the same route to work. I know every twist, turn, and traffic constraint. I know exactly how long it takes me to get from home to work. I could probably drive it with my eyes closed. One morning, I encountered a detour. Although directional signs were posted, I struggled to trust that I would not get lost. I was not comfortable deviating from my norm to take a longer and out-of-the-way route. I panicked and then became frustrated. I did not plan for the extra time to take an alternate route. The alternate route was a narrow two-lane road with little traffic. I feared assistance would not come quickly if I got lost in this unfamiliar territory or my car broke down. After a bout of apprehension, I decided to trust the detour. I bypassed construction and made it to work with only a ten-minute delay.

Numbers 22 is the story of Prophet Balaam. The Moabites asked him to curse the Israelites, but God told him to bless them instead. In an attempt to bribe him, the Moabites offered the prophet a promotion and great honor. He accepted. Angered by his action, the Lord had other plans. As Balaam traveled with the princes of Moab, the donkey he rode detoured into a field. Up the road, the donkey saw an angel with its sword drawn and tried to avoid it. Unable to see the spiritual being, Balaam hit the donkey three times. The Lord opened the donkey's mouth, and she had a conversation with Balaam. God opened Balaam's eyes, he saw the angel, and acknowledged that he had sinned against God. Blinded by his own agenda, Balaam could not see the detour designed to redirect him to the will of God.

God instructed Jonah to go to Nineveh. He was commissioned to tell the people that He saw their wickedness and was not pleased. Jonah chose to take an alternate route because he knew the power of God's word and did not want the responsibility of carrying it. His disobedience landed him in the belly of a big fish for three days and nights. In the midst of partially digested food, stomach bile, and other disgusting things, Jonah prayed. The Lord spoke to the fish, and it vomited Jonah onto dry land. Jonah rerouted to his original assignment and made a three-day journey in one day. Run, Jonah! Run.

Don't get so comfortable with the familiar, that you miss the detours. Although it may seem longer to get to the destination, you'll never know what perils, pitfalls, and potholes you avoided by following God's detours.

> *Then the Lord opened Balaam's eyes, and he saw the Angel of the Lord standing in the way with His drawn sword in His hand; and he bowed his head and fell flat on his face. And Balaam said to the Angel of the Lord, "I have sinned, for I did not know You*

stood in the way against me. Now therefore, if it displeases You, I will turn back."
—Numbers 22: 31, 34

The steps of a good man are ordered by the Lord, and He delights in his way.
—Psalm 37:23

A man's heart plans his way, but the Lord directs his steps.
—Proverbs 16:9

Reflection Activity

Reflect on detours you experienced that got you to your destination later than expected.

_____

_____

_____

_____

_____

LaToya D. Masterson

Why were the detours necessary?

_____

_____

_____

_____

What did you avoid with the detours?

_____

_____

_____

_____

Did the detours change your destination?

_____

_____

_____

_____

Day 28

Most Needful

Distractions keep you from giving full attention to needful matters and hinder what you are trying to accomplish. As daily tasks and obligations grow, everything becomes a priority, but nothing seems to get done.

I attended a prioritization workshop. The facilitator asked us to identify the "big rocks" — aka important things — that aligned with our life goals. My top three were faith, family, and friends; however, I was so busy being busy that I was distracted from what was most needful. After the workshop, I stepped back from the day-to-day busyness to prioritize my faith, family, and friends. I dedicated time to pray, fast, and read the Word to feed my faith. To invest in relationships, I have Sunday dinners with family and occasional Saturday outings. I am intentional about calling or texting regularly.

When Jesus visited Martha's home, she was preoccupied with serving her guests. Her sister, Mary, sat at Jesus's feet and listened to Him. Bothered that her sister was not helping her, Martha asked Jesus, "Do You not care that she left me alone to serve?" Jesus said, "You are careful and troubled about many things; but one thing is needful and Mary hath chosen that good part which shall not be taken away from her." Not that Martha's work wasn't of value, but Mary recognized that being in the presence of God was most important.

Whether social media, TV, or a person to whom you are attracted, identify distractions that keep you from progressing. Be intentional about prioritizing needful things by scheduling them; otherwise, they will fall to the bottom of your to-do pile.

> *And He said, "My Presence will go with you, and I will give you rest."*
> —Exodus 33:14

> *You will show me the path of life; in Your presence is fullness of joy; at Your right hand are pleasures forevermore.*
> —Psalm 16:11

> *For in Him we live and move and have our being, as also some of your own poets have said, 'For we are also His offspring.'*
> —Acts 17:28

Reflection Activity

Read Luke 10:38-42. What did you learn about worship, service, and needful things?

_____

_____

_____

_____

_____

Identify the top three things that are the most important to you.

_____

_____

_____

_____

_____

How have you been distracted from making those things top priority?

_____
_____
_____
_____
_____

What steps can you take to eliminate the distractions?

_____
_____
_____
_____
_____

Day 29

Ready or Not, Here I Come

I loved to play Hide-n-Seek with friends. We enjoyed hours of fun finding the best hiding places and outrunning the "seeker" to home base. We played indoors and outdoors but had the most fun outdoors because of the endless hiding places. I preferred to hide because I devised a fail-proof strategy. Keeping my eyes on the seeker, I hid in a camouflaged space not too far from base. When the seeker counted down, said, "Ready or not, here I come," and left base looking for hiders, I sprinted home. Safe!

The parable of the ten virgins reminded me of this childhood game because winning required preparation and awareness of surroundings. The bridegroom arrived unannounced one evening. Although all the virgins had lamps, only five were prepared with oil. The foolish virgins tried to convince the wise ones to give them oil. When that didn't work, they ran to buy oil. While they were gone, the bridegroom took the prepared virgins with him to the marriage feast. Lack of preparation caused the five foolish virgins to miss out. Ready or not, the bridegroom is coming. Will you be ready?

Many of the end-time signs Jesus mentioned in Matthew 24:3-8 have happened. Are you ready for His return? Time out for getting ready, you have to be ready. Christ wants you to be like Him. When you hide His Word in your heart, and seek Him with all your might, you will fill your lamp.

> *"Ask, and it will be given to you; seek, and you will find; knock, and it will be opened to you. For everyone who asks receives, and he who seeks finds, and to him who knocks it will be opened."*
> —Matthew 7:7-8

> *Therefore you also be ready, for the Son of Man is coming at an hour you do not expect.*
> —Matthew 24:44

> *"Now when these things begin to happen, look up and lift up your heads, because your redemption draws near."*
> —Luke 21:28

Reflection Activity

Read the parable of the virgins in Matthew 25:1-13. What are your thoughts after reading this passage?

_____

_____

_____

_____

_____

How can you prepare yourself as the bride of Christ?

_____

_____

_____

_____

LaToya D. Masterson

Day 30

I AM THAT I AM

I grew up in the church and often heard stories of how others experienced God. In Sunday school, I learned that He healed the blind, deaf, and lame. He fed 5,000 with five fish and two loaves of bread and raised a man from the dead.

As I matured, I had personal experiences with God that shaped my knowledge of Him. At sixteen, I worked the late shift at a movie theater on weekends. After the last show started, I cleared the popcorn machine, swept the floor, and prepared to close concessions. I counted my drawer and knelt to place the money in the drop box under the counter. When I stood, the barrel of a gun was pointed at my face. My heart raced. Paralyzed with fear, I heard a man in the distance screaming but could not make out his words. He yanked open a theater door and I ran toward him. I ran to the front of the theater and warned the customers to duck in their seats. About twenty minutes later, a male customer led us out the theater. The robber was nowhere in sight. I'm not sure if running into the theater was a smart thing to do, but through that experience, I know God as my present help, protector, and preserver.

God raised up Moses to deliver the children of Israel from Pharaoh's bondage. When God called him to do the work, Moses gave several excuses:

- Who am I that You chose me to approach Pharaoh?
- When the children of Israel ask who sent me, what name do I give them?
- What if they don't believe me?
- I don't speak well. Moses had a speech impediment and tried to use it to disqualify himself.
- Send someone else.

With each excuse, God provided a solution to fulfill His promise to Abraham (Genesis 12:1-3). When Moses asked who was sending him, God said, "Tell them that I AM sent you."

God's name is I AM, not I was, or I might be. In my reflection time, I hear God say, "I AM your healer. I AM your deliverer. I AM your very present help. I AM your strong tower. I AM your comforter. I AM your way maker. I AM your sustainer. I AM your heart fixer. I AM your mind regulator. I AM your strength."

Nothing is more rewarding than serving a God who loves me more than I could ever love myself. He is all that I will ever need, and He desires to be that for you. If you are going to reign with Him, you will experience suffering. No one is exempt from the trials of life but be encouraged. You serve the I AM God, and He will come to your rescue.

And God said to Moses, "I AM WHO I AM." And He said, "Thus you shall say to the children of Israel, 'I AM has sent me to you.'"
—Exodus 3:14

And you are complete in Him, who is the head of all principality and power.
—Colossians 2:10

If we endure, we shall also reign with Him. If we deny Him, He also will deny us.
—2 Timothy 2:12

Reflection Activity

Read Exodus 3. Reflect on the chapter. What three things come to mind?

_____

_____

_____

_____

_____

Write I AM statements that describe who you are in God.

_____

_____

_____

_____

_____

How has spending time in the Word and prayer strengthened your relationship with God?

_____

_____

_____

_____

_____

About LaToya D. Masterson

Her profession is nursing; her passion is nurturing.

Using her life as a model of lessons learned overcoming adversity, discrimination, and exclusion, LaToya D. Masterson influences women to trust God, never quit, and pursue dreams. As a certified John C. Maxwell coach, trainer, and speaker, she trains women in leadership, personal development, and the importance of adding value to others.

Blessed with mentors who guided her to navigate personal and professional challenges, she vowed to give back by mentoring young ladies to build solid relationships. As Naomi cultivated Ruth, LaToya sows seeds of integrity, authenticity, and expectation to help blossoming leaders reap their God-ordained harvest. As an ordained minister, she is a resource who plants, waters, and prepares the soul for God's increase.

For speaking engagements, workshops, and bulk purchases of *Mastering Me*, contact LaToya at info@latoyadmasterson.com or visit LaToyaDMasterson.com.

LaToya D. Masterson

About Queen V Publishing

The Doorway to YOUR Destiny!

Go thou and publish abroad the kingdom of God.

—Luke 9:60 ESV

Committed to transforming manuscripts into polished works of art, **Queen V Publishing** is a company of standard and integrity. We offer an alternative that allows the message in YOU to do what it was sent to do for OTHERS.

QueenVPublishing.com

Serving professional speakers and experts to magnify and monetize their message by publishing quality books

LaToya D. Masterson

www.ingramcontent.com/pod-product-compliance
Lightning Source LLC
Chambersburg PA
CBHW070912080526
44589CB00013B/1272